BRITAIN IN PICTURES
THE BRITISH PEOPLE IN PICTURES

THE STORY OF IRELAND

GENERAL EDITOR

W. J. TURNER

★

The Editor is most grateful to all those who have
so kindly helped in the selection of illustrations,
especially to officials of the various public
Museums, Libraries and Galleries, and
to all others who have generously
allowed pictures and MSS.
to be reproduced.

THE
STORY OF IRELAND

SEAN O'FAOLAIN

WITH
8 PLATES IN COLOUR
AND
22 ILLUSTRATIONS IN
BLACK & WHITE

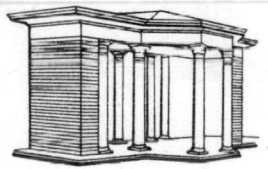

WILLIAM COLLINS OF LONDON
MCMXXXXIII

PRODUCED BY

ADPRINT LIMITED LONDON

★

PRINTED

IN GREAT BRITAIN

LIST OF ILLUSTRATIONS

PLATES IN COLOUR

BLACK & WHITE ILLUSTRATIONS

BRIEF HISTORICAL CHRONOLOGY

A.D.

5th Century. Patricius comes to Ireland

8th Century. Norse Attacks begin

1169 Beginnings of Norman Invasion

1367 Statute of Kilkenny marks Norman
absorption

1495 Poynings' Laws limit powers of Dublin
Parliament

1535 Henry VIII's Reformation Com-
mission

1569-1583 Desmond Wars

1594-1603 Hugh O'Neill in arms

1641-1652 Stuart and Cromwellian Wars

1685-1691 Williamite Wars

1697-1746 The Penal Code

A.D.

1757 Catholic Committee Founded

1782 Legislative Independence of Dublin
Parliament

1801 Union of Ireland and Great Britain
in a single Parliament

1823 Daniel O'Connell founds Catholic
Association

1829 Catholic Emancipation

1845-1848 Famine Period. Growth of
Young Ireland movement

1875 Parnell enters Parliament

1879 The Land League founded

1906 Arthur Griffith founds his paper *Sinn
Fein*

1922 The Irish Free State is founded

THE ROCK OF CASHEL
Water colour by W. H. Bartlett, 1809 - 1854

IF one looks at a map of the world Ireland appears as an island of moderate size—it is smaller than Java or Cuba, and its population is minute: about four million—on the extreme west of the continent of Europe. It is so close to the continent, and, one knows, so closely bound to the history of Britain, that one as naturally takes it to be as much part of Europe as, say, at least Sardinia or Crete. On closer examination it seems much more tightly bound to the modern world than either of these. On the map the blue threads of ocean-routes draw it, by its proximity to the Port of London, close to the centre of a vast web of commerce and civilisation. The colour-masses on the map which indicate a community of languages, religions, and political associations, emphasise this sense of Ireland's central position and European connection. Nevertheless Ireland's remote position has given her a curious degree of detachment from the modern world; so much so in certain ways that she might be as remote as Iceland. Indeed an Irishman is sometimes so acutely aware of this detachment that he may wonder whether his island does not adhere to, rather than belong to Europe; and, as he glances back at the story of his little island, he will probably feel that much of it was dictated by this ambiguity in her relationship to the rest of the world.

7

MAP OF IRELAND
Drawn by F. Nichols

Even the casual traveller to Ireland will make this discovery very quickly for himself. He will cross from Britain to Dublin or to Belfast on the East Coast, and, at first, since Ireland is hinged most firmly to Europe at these two points, find little that is not familiar, and have no sense of provincialism. There is an atmosphere of profitable commerce about the shipyards and factories of Belfast, and a tradition of metropolitan dignity and opulence still glows from the slightly decrepit Georgian face of Dublin. In Dublin he will find, if in no great number, the ordinary amenities of any capital city: shops, galleries, universities, theatres, continental food, and the nucleus of a pleasant and cultivated society. He will expect that some things, memories, and citizens of that city should have a world-repute and he will find them. They will be thrust upon him. James Joyce, Parnell, Swift, Guinness, the Rotunda Medical School, Jacob's Biscuits, Oscar Wilde (or rather his father, Sir William and his mother, "Speranza"), the Abbey Theatre, Yeats, Dublin University, Michael Collins, Boss Croker, Goldsmith, innumerable anonymous "characters," many wits, and a few distinguished admirals and generals such as Wellington or the two Goughs. He will hear of patriots and lost causes by the score. Obviously a city that has been for a long time trafficked by the world: adult, busy, sophisticated. That aura which a city can only acquire by a long and varied experience of contemporary life hangs over Dublin. Like the hero of Meredith's *The Egoist* who "had a leg," Dublin has an air.

But it cannot be very long (perhaps an hour will do) before the traveller begins to form some reservations. He soon realises that there are two clocks in Dublin. Some might say—of this world and the next; it is going far enough to say—of to-day and a very far-off yesterday. He will soon come up against an attitude to life that he will call either traditional or antiquated; venerable or primitive, according to his philosophy. Of this attitude to life the signs are various. Business is taken at a pace which, according to mood, seems either leisurely and pleasant, or maddeningly inefficient. Beggars are distressingly common, and importunate. There are very few *chic* women. Sophistication is confined to a minute central section of three or four streets. Religious emblems are everywhere, in shops, crumpled on the dashboard of the taxi, pinned behind the door of the hotel, in a shrine in the centre of the principal street and, in the middle of the busy morning, crowds will pour out of a church in a side-street, and the evenings are melodious with bells. There is a slum, as it will seem at first, around every corner. The whole place has an air of Lilliput. And the key to it all is down on the docks among the moving cattle. What is hinged to Europe, that is to say, is a small, pastoral and agricultural country whose main exports are livestock, hams, bacon, eggs, whisky, stout, agricultural and dairy produce. The wonder is how so modern a city ever came out of so traditional a life.

For Dublin or Belfast are of 1943: but an hour out of Belfast are the Antrim Glens, and an hour out of Dublin are the Wicklow mountains, or the great central plain with its vast peat-bogs, and there, as on a ship, according as the traveller goes farther and farther west, he puts back his watch—but here one puts it back

9

not by hours but by centuries. Away down on the wild and jagged coast of Kerry, or over on the tattered fragments of Connemara, it is the Middle Ages.

I doubt if one could possibly arrange a tour of any extent for a visitor during which he would not feel this tug-of-war between modernity and tradition. For one thing the mere fact that the country is now entirely English-speaking—one would have to search very hard for a man who could not speak English—leads one to expect a uniformity with the rest of the English-speaking world. If this casual expectation is satisfied on one's first experience, in the capital, if it is not already shaken by such signs as I have mentioned, it would be utterly shattered were the visitor to Dublin to do no more than cycle over the Wicklow hills, down by Glenmacnass, into the antique cul-de-sac of Glendalough. Around here we are in a country of small, mountainy farms, poor soil, cows straying by the road, and sheep bleating in the fog. The dramatist Synge put it all into a play like *The Shadow of the Glen*, several of his poems, one of his prose-books. It savours of a folk-world. Yet we are only thirty-three miles from Dublin.

It is like changing gloaming into a gradual daylight to drive on down to the rich counties of Carlow and Kilkenny, parts of which are as urbane as Buckinghamshire or Hertfordshire, with stately homes, thriving towns, "big" farms (say two hundred acres), rich soil, fine woods. And if the traveller stood in the grey age of Kilkenny city—one of the oldest cities in Ireland—and then radiated out in any direction for sixty miles, he would find the same enviable countryside; and know, incidentally, why the Normans invaded this island.

But if he should go on, following the River Nore to Waterford, and then strike west around or through the mountains of West Waterford and Tipperary and North Cork—still finding much but not such consistently fine land on his way—by degrees, he will feel the twilight fall again. There, west of the Galtees, in North Cork, is where the poet Spenser was planted, under Elizabeth, and where he wrote a portion of *The Faerie Queene*. The memory of that shadowy, flickering, dusky poem will be in accord with the life about him. If he were to pursue the circuit of Ireland it would be like that all the way, diving from Time to Time like a dolphin. It is largely an economic matter. The poor lands are, by history, linked to the centuries when the natives were driven out of the profitable lands: in hardship they retained, and have atavistically retained to this day, the traditions of the life they lost. Here one gets the twenty-five acre farms raising families of six, eight, or ten children.

So, our traveller on this typical tour would find another modern thriving town at Mallow, dive into the underworld again, west of it, as he approaches the stern, mountainous country about Killarney—too tourist-ridden now to be more than a series of magnificent views; and should he then continue westward down the northern side of Dingle Bay, to the Gaelic-speaking patch around Slea Head, or to the wild Blasket Island, he will no longer doubt that this mingling of the centuries is a characteristic of Ireland. This is the romantic Ireland: romantic to the traveller who is not obliged to live there. Though, perhaps, the truer word is not "live," but "exist."

GALWAY PEASANTS
Wash drawing by Augustus John

Come out of Kerry up to the Shannon. The planes are alighting at Foynes, from Botwood, maybe ten a day. County Limerick yields prize-crops and breeds prize horses. But now cross the Shannon to stony Clare and, if you know your modern Irish literature, you will recall those little plays of Lady Gregory, like *The Gaol Gate*, or *Spreading the News*, which have taken from local life the mellowness of a folk-tale and the simplicity of a miracle-play. Galway city reeks of the 16th century under its thin layer of paint and chromium. The Gaelic-speaking Aran Islands, out on the ever-grey ocean, are primaeval. Connemara, Mayo, Sligo are foreign-looking through being so patriarchally native. Life here is cruelly hard: farms as small as ten bad acres rearing very large families, most of them doomed to emigrate. Fishing ekes out a poor existence but were it not for emigration and Government support much of this country would be un-inhabitable. Yet, in every town along the way—Clifden, Castlebar, or Ballina, you may, of course, spend the nights with Hollywood, or anywhere accidentally bump into people as contemporaneous as Fleet Street, and less superficial.

Sligo—which is the Yeats country—is the most extravagant contrast of age and youth, poverty and comfort, century and century. When you are coming out of Donegal you find two little towns, Lifford and Strabane, on either side of a river, and of a Customs Border (between Eire and the Six Counties) whose comparison might be the text for Ireland's unresolved variety. After that you are in the Six Counties where the present is inescapable, and as you felt no jar in arriving in Dublin from London, you may, without a jar, cross back from clanging Belfast to clanging Glasgow. If you should complete the circuit back to Dublin you will, on the last lap, touch pre-history at the monolithic monuments of New Grange and at Tara, and dine that evening in a restaurant as good as any in the world.

The explanation for these contrasts is, as I have suggested, almost wholly economic. The economic set-up in Ireland has, for long, been that of a once-depressed race gradually re-establishing its fortunes. Once the colonists prospered, and the natives became poorer and poorer; then the tide turned (from about 1850 on) and the colonists began to drift, and the natives began to make headway. The gradation of these contrasts, which every traveller observes, corresponds to this ebb and flow of fortune. If we note the two great links between Ireland and the outer world we shall see a clear illustration of this. Those links are economic and cultural. They explain the anomaly of Dublin; and of modernism rising everywhere in little sunny atolls out of a mist of tradition.

On the economic plane forced emigration reduced the then utterly depressed population of Ireland, in the mid-19th century, by almost four million. The emigrants went chiefly to America, but also in numbers to Britain. Curiously they never work on the land abroad: they adapt themselves immediately to city-life. That drain on man-power was born of hardship (the result of conquest)—it was hastened by Famine (the result of misgovernment). Nevertheless it had a profitable reaction in so far as the standard of living of the remainder rose perceptibly: there was a little more money and a little more living-room. Just before this War it was found that two of the three great credit items of Ireland's finance were naval, military, and police pensions (from Britain), and emigrants' remittances (from America). Political reforms increased the prosperity of the farmer all through the 19th century. That emigrant link is between depression at home and prosperity abroad. It is both temporal and spatial. Everything in

12

CLIFDEN, COUNTY GALWAY
Oil painting by Stephen Bone

Ireland is. There is, as yet, no static Now in Ireland. There is nothing mystical or Celtic Twilight-ish about this. In any country where the social and economic order becomes a battle-ground the fluctuations of fortune infect all life with their own uncertainty as to both the present and the future.

On the cultural plane we meet the more fortunate—whether they are of colonist or native stock. These Irishmen have built up a great physical and spiritual traffic with the world, somewhat of necessity but mainly by a natural desire to share in a world-community of intellect. That traffic has been persistent and unbroken ever since the 17th century. It has been most striking since the 18th century, which began the great flow of writers and students of every kind to London. One thinks of them at random: Thomas Amory; Henry Brooks; Sheridan; Goldsmith. Sometimes these men went out of Ireland and did not return: sometimes they did return: sometimes they stayed at home and exported and imported ideas. Robert Boyle, the famous chemist and philosopher (1627-1691), was born in the County Waterford but settled in Oxford when he was twenty-four. William Harvey, the botanist, (1811-1866) left Ireland for Capetown,

13

but returned early and did all his work in Dublin. Wallace, the composer, (1814-1865) had finished his musical education in Dublin before travelling the world. Edward Hincks (1792 - 1866), a Corkman, was an Egyptologist of European fame who did all his work in an obscure village in County Down. Edward Dowden (1843 - 1913) enriched Shakespearian scholarship from a lifetime in Dublin University. One could string out this list to an impressive length—Berkeley, whose thought still affects contemporary philosophy, Swift, Burke, Hamilton, of whom Einstein said that he owed much to Hamilton's mathematical genius, down to Wilde, Shaw, T. E. Lawrence, George Moore, Yeats, James Stephens, or Lord Dunsany. Most of these belong to the more or less well-off colonists who built up this graceful ruby-brick 18th century core of the city of Dublin that stretches from Mountjoy Square in the North to Merrion Square in the South, and many pleasant houses and "seats" in the suburbs. Many of them were quite poor men. Sheridan, for example, was the son of an actor.

There are other names of distinguished men who have passed through this island on their journey to immortality and left their humane mark upon it. They represent the less fortunate native on the upgrade. The delicate statue of Oliver Goldsmith, outside Trinity College in Dublin, reminds us of one, the sculptor Foley. The bust of James Clarence Mangan, the poet, in Saint Stephen's Green, reminds us of another. The novelist Carleton was a farmer's son; the two Banims were also farmer stock; Tom Moore; the painter Maclise; the journalist Maginn; Goldsmith's colleague, the dramatist Kelly, was a publican's son—and here one thinks of a host of those Irish strugglers and stragglers of Oliver's seedy days; the painter Barry; the great Daniel O'Connell; the Celtic scholar, John O'Donovan; the orator, Richard Lalor Shiel; John Fitzgibbon, Earl of Clare, and Lord Chancellor of Ireland, was the grandson of a peasant-farmer; and so on, by the hundred, down to our own day and to such names as Sean O'Casey, James Joyce, or Liam O'Flaherty.

Put both lists of names together, colonist and native, and one realises that, however hateful and unjust the invasion of Ireland was to the native, the blending of two races and cultures finally brought about an interesting and vital mentality. The contrasts and the varieties and the complexities have here gradually become assimilated into a unified race of astonishing productivity.

One would say that modern Ireland has stabilised herself on that blending, if there were not some Irishmen, to-day, who fear and even resent the world-traffic that has resulted from it. They would like to turn the clock back and begin all over again, as if the entire process of historical fusion had never occurred, and could be obliterated. They feel that the national identity is in danger from a world-traffic of this order, and are attempting to found a philosophy of self-sufficiency on seclusionism, based on the revival of the Gaelic language, the rise of a Catholic ascendancy, and the elimination, whereever possible, of the English tongue. (This is Celtophilism, one should say, and not Anglophobia.) Others, perhaps the majority, feel that these idealists do not realise the good-fortune of their country, and can never have compared it with the fate of other small

JAMES JOYCE, 1882 - 1941
Pencil drawing by Augustus John

countries, buried in Europe, and insulated from easy viability. Thus, in a country
like Hungary, there is such a bottled-up surplus of professional men that Doctors-
at-Law become bus-conductors, and to share in the world-community so wide
open to us requires collossal effort, and is only achieved by comparatively few.
But this is a controversial subject, to be found also in Scotland and Wales, though
not so acute in those countries because they have not independent parliaments.

One would have to go to South Africa to find a closer parallel, and, possibly, a forecast of the outcome.

There is one great economic factor in Ireland which helps to consolidate the traditional, or patriarchal life-modes and to retard the modernists. I have mentioned it, in passing. Ireland has no heavy industries outside the shipyards in the city of Belfast. There are no great industrial or commercial cities to absorb the surplus of the fields and the population is so small that their needs never can develop such great cities. So, in the North of Ireland, it has been noted, emigration to America has never been so severe as in the south because the children may go to Belfast, to business or to factory: but in the south of Ireland, outside Dublin, the "cities" are really just large towns. The traditionalism of Irish rural life is not therefore challenged by Irish urban sophistication. Yet—it may well be that this absence of cities and heavy industry may work in quite another way; the stronger challenge may come from outside. That is to say that emigration may be persistent and uncontrollable, and that the countryside will then either be enriched by this constant communication and blending (mainly, of course, with Great Britain), or, drained of its most adventurous blood, sink into torpor. The whole trend, as shewn by recent Census returns, is from the fields into the towns, and from the towns into Dublin, and the war has caused an enormous amount of emigration to Great Britain.

Thus, when all is said and done, what the perspicuous visitor to Dublin and traveller in Ireland will really observe is the clash that naturally results when an old, small, and not powerful country meets the powerful impact of modern life. That impact comes on Ireland from east and from west. She is in the mid-stream of the flow between America and Europe. Those planes alighting out of the sky from America at Foynes, and those planes taking off into the sky to Britain, are the symbols of this contest. But, surely, it is an old story? Many countries have had the same experience—Turkey, Greece, Egypt, China. To understand it fully one must read the political and social history of each country, and that we must now, in turn, do with Ireland.

THE early history of Ireland falls into three parts: the pre-Christian, heroic period of the great epics and sagas; the great creative, evangelistic period of early Irish Christianity—that is, from the 5th to 9th century—to which Irishmen still look back with pride; and the centuries following the Norman invasion, on whose conclusion (i.e. around 1400), the formative history of modern Ireland may be said to begin.

The early pre-Christian centuries are fabular, and Anglo-Irish literature of the last sixty years has made them familiar—in the heroic plays of Yeats, such as *On Baile's Strand*, or in Synge's *Deirdre*, or in Yeats's poems, such as *The Wanderings of Usheen*. The later centuries from the 5th to the 9th are best recaptured in translations of Old Gaelic lyrics by Kuno Meyer, Robin Flower or

ST. MARK

Illumination from the *Book of Kells*, 8th century

BRICKEEN BRIDGE BETWEEN FORE LAKE AND THE GREAT LAKE, KILLARNEY

Coloured aquatint by S. Alken after T. Walmesley

KERRY CASTLE
Water colour by Cornelius Varley, 1842

Frank O'Connor; or in their great triumphs the Book of Durrow, or the Gospels of Lindisfarne, or the Book of Kells (7th to 9th century), which are among the finest illuminated manuscripts in the world. That period of Irish spiritual and cultural influence all over the continent broke on the Norse invasions (8th to 11th century). The mark of those centuries, to-day, on the landscape are the Round Towers, or those clusters of picturesque little Celtic churches, in ruins, to which one pays pilgrimage in remote places like Glendalough, or Clonmacnoise. After that comes the period of the Norman invasion. Those ruined square towers that one sees from the train sticking up out of the meadowlands like broken teeth, inhabited only by the cattle sheltering from the sun or the storm are relics of that prolonged struggle.

The essential facts about the history of that third period (12th to 14th century) are that under the old Gaelic tradition political unity was never lastingly achieved, and that the Norman conquest was, as such, a failure since the Normans were ultimately absorbed into the disorder which made their invasion possible. Thus, modern Irish names like Fitzgerald, Costello, Cogan, Burke, Hackett, Barry, Roche are all of Norman origin.

Here the ambiguity of Ireland's relationship with Britain and Europe already becomes apparent. The Norman conquest was directed from London

17

ANCIENT CROSS AND ROUND TOWER, CLONMACNOISE
Engraving from *The Scenery and Antiquities of Ireland*, 1842

but was never properly controlled. Had Ireland either been a thousand miles from London, or just twenty, the result would have been far different. Had she been as near as Wales, London would have attended to the business of organising the results of the invasion; had she been a thousand miles away she would probably have attended to her own affairs, undisturbed. She would, that is, have been able to develop out of a semi-feudal, semi-Celtic disjunction into a centralised state.

Even as it was this organisation was within Ireland's grasp. The invaders had already set up the anatomy of a central government in Dublin, with a parliament, a viceroy, a few officials, an advisory council. It is true that these laws were for those of Anglo-Norman blood alone, but desuetude or reform could have adapted them to custom or tradition; and, in any case, they had little force in practice since it was Gaelic custom that dominated the lives of the vast majority of the people. Instead of mingling Gaelic custom and Norman law this local "centre" limped on ineffectively until the time of the Tudors, contributing little or nothing to Ireland's essential need for political unification and organisation, and all London did was to interfere when it found that the Normans were becoming Gaelicised. The key-date, there, is 1366—when certain laws called The Statutes of Kilkenny sought in vain to restrain the colonists from adopting Irish ways.

IONA CATHEDRAL, SHOWING A CELTIC CROSS
Lithograph from H. D. Graham's *Antiquities of Iona*, 1850

This failure of the Norman Conquest in Ireland is one of the pivotal points of our history. One would regret it the less—indeed not regret it at all—if the Gaelic system had been capable of central government: it had, instead, been disintegrating for so long that it is impossible to say when the disintegration began. It had not been a coherent or virile thing since, at least, the 12th century. In the period following the Norman invasion it kept gradually fraying away and away into a condition that was almost anarchical. Dynastic ambition became its key-note, internecine rivalry its habit of life, and it is plain that the Gaelic chieftains had, in effect, begun to alter more and more towards that feudalism which they originally opposed, and that this disturbance of the seeds of whatever possibility of development there was in the pure Gaelic system completely stopped its growth. But, possibly, it may be suggested, the element of Adaptability was never in it? Possibly that system was suited only to the uncomplex conditions of those heroic and candid times for which it was created? Whatever the reason, inherent or extraneous, the Gaelic system held far less promise than the Norman-Gaelic, and most of its later story, therefore, is desultory, and pointless, and of purely local interest.

And whatever else is debatable now, or unpredictable then, about this middle-period of Irish history the one thing which is certain is that any Irishman whose outlook was purely local might as well be said to have had no outlook at all. For with the coming to power of the Tudors, Ireland was becoming important in world-affairs for the first time in her long life. In the destiny of the Lancastrians to found a great dynasty, and their fear of Dublin as a Yorkist cell, (to use a modern word): in the destiny of England to be a great world-empire that would challenge the empire of Spain and need every possible outpost of defence; in the destiny of Europe to be riven by the great spiritual controversies of the Reformation and Counter-Reformation which would leave no remotest island untouched by their fires, Ireland was to find herself the battle-ground of a complex of ideas, ambitions, rivalries, against which her innate conservatism and traditionalism were to tear themselves for hundreds of years. The mediaeval world was at an end. The world of the Renaissance, with all its vigour, all its ruthlessness, all its explosive, destructive, and creative power, was stretching out its hand to the very ends of the world. Long ago one of those Irish *deoraidhe*, or wanderers, the saintly Cummian, with his mind on the order of Rome, the civilisation of the Hellenised East, the image of a great uniform Church, had looked about him at his people (then refusing obstinately to conform to the practice of the universal Church in the famous Paschal controversy), and in anger he had cried—"So, Rome is in error, Jerusalem is in error, Alexandria is in error, Antioch is in error: the Irish and Britons alone have true wisdom!"— and spoke of Ireland as *mentagrae orbis terrarum*, a pimple on the chin of the world. Her story from this on is just as obstinate, but the obstinacy now revolves around an intellectual idea, and because of that her story is of universal interest.

This way of regarding the failure of the Norman Conquest of Ireland as a tragic thing might not appeal to every modern Irishman. We have been brought up to look at our history rather too much in the light of the last two or three hundred years, seeing it as a straightforward fight between Eire as the heroine and England as the ruthless villain. England was certainly ruthless from the day that Henry Tudor seriously set himself to win control of this neighbouring island—possibly even more ruthless than any other country in that ruthless time when "total war" became a fact for the first time in history. But it was not merely England that pressed down on us. It was the whole weight of world-forces then accumulating to press heavily on every country in the world. Moreover, if history is the record of human striving towards a fruitful and ordered society, then every problem is a problem not of nationality but of civilisation, and events have a lasting significance only as they are part of that process. From this viewpoint we may say that the Celt succeeded for a time, but that, by the highest test, his civilisation proved abortive. The Norman gave some promise of creating a new order, but he, also, did not succeed. The subsequent amalgamation of Norman and Gaelic failed dismally. We now are to watch the Tudors attempt it in bloodshed and cruelty so prolonged and so pitiless, and so hardily resisted, that it became plain, in time, that those wars of conquest were, in effect, wars of utter extermination. And, it appears, whatever the most cruel wars can do in the way of destruction—their chief purpose and main pursuit—the one achievement beyond their power is to annihilate a people.

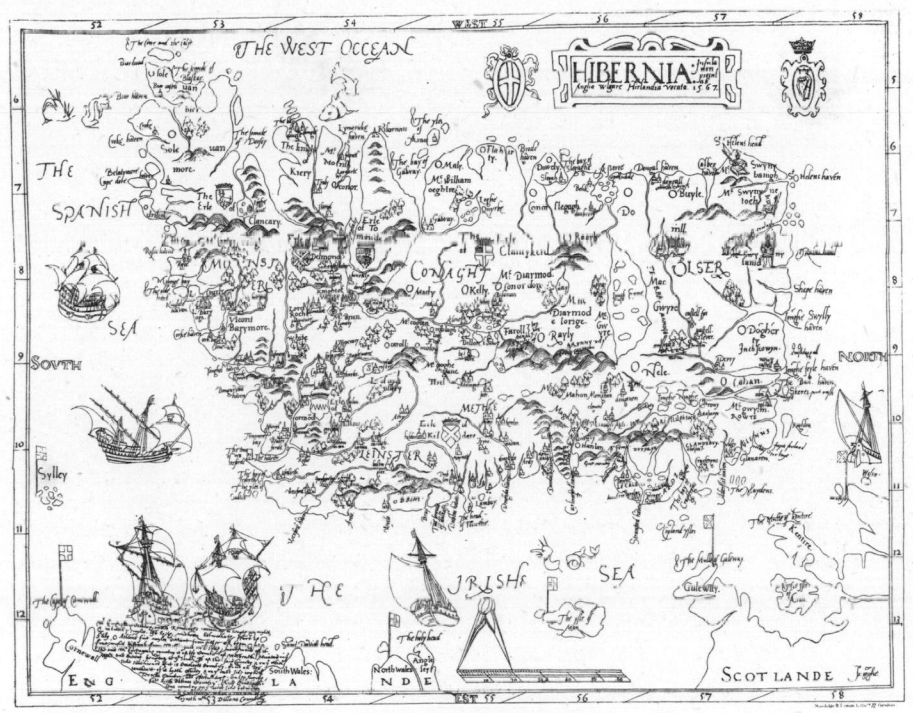

MAP OF IRELAND, 1567
Centemporary tinted drawing

A S the essential date for the end of the Norman effort at the complete conquest of Ireland is 1366, the essential date for the beginning of the Tudor "reconquest" is 1494 - 5. In December, 1494, a Parliament was called in Dublin by a new Deputy, Sir Edward Poynings, whose name was for ever to be associated with the laws passed at that Parliament and known collectively as "Poynings' Act." That "Act" laid it down that all laws lately passed in England should be valid for Ireland, and came to mean, in time, *all* laws, even those passed long previously. Moreover no Bills could be laid before the Dublin Parliament until sanction had been given by the King and Privy Council. Anything that had existed in the way of Norman-Gaelic "Home Rule" in Ireland was thus, on paper, destroyed at a blow. Poynings' Act was, in short, on paper, a 15th century Act of Union. One insists on the words "on paper", however, because such an Act—indeed any Act passed by this puppet parliament in Dublin—could have no force until force established it far and wide over the country, so that Poynings' Act is, in effect, a kind of blue-print for the ruthless wars that followed. These

21

wars did not end until the close of the 17th century with that exodus to the continent of the last of the native aristocracy which is known to Irish history as the Flight of the Wild Geese.

Here Religion once again becomes the fiery cross of Irish idealism. In the Reformation Parliament of England, 1529 - 1536, Henry VIII broke with Rome. In 1541 two Jesuits, the apostles of the counter-attack, visited Ireland. At that date the main struggle may conveniently be said to begin. It would, however, be quite wrong to propose that Religion inspired the struggle on the English side. On the contrary, it was the Irish who identified their resistance to Tudor aggression with the idealism of the Counter-Reformation; or, it might be more accurate to say that they were encouraged to do so by the emissaries of Spain and Rome who saw in Ireland the opportunity for a flank attack on Britain. The Tudor revival of interest in Ireland was part of the traditional zeal of the adventurer-colonist, part of a natural process of expansion westward, and it was also dictated by fear of invasion from the continent. The religious motive entered gradually and ambiguously, its progress retarded on the side of the colonists by their military weakness which could not, or dared not enforce widely the new decrees relating to religion, and retarded on the side of the Gaelic chiefs and the Norman-Irish houses, like the Geraldines (Kildare and Desmond), by a disunity which made each man temporise for as long as he and his were left in comparative peace. In any case religion in Ireland, in the first half of the 16th century, was anything but a brilliant light.

Henry VIII proceeded cautiously, and his masterpiece of diplomatic strategy was the policy known as "Surrender and Re-grant." By this all that was required of the Gaelic chiefs was to acknowledge the supremacy of the Crown, surrender their lands to it, and receive them back as lieges of the King. This proposal was so plausible, and seemed so harmless, that most of the great native chiefs accepted it easily. Thus the western Burkes (originally Norman de Burgos) became Earls of Clanrickarde; the northern O'Neills became Earls of Tyrone; the southern O'Briens became Earls of Thomond; Manus O'Donnell, in the north-west, agreed to take a title of the same order. Not until the death of Elizabeth, however, did an O'Donnell actually receive the title of Earl of Tyrconnell. Overtly this nominal feudalisation did not at first appear to make much difference—obviously custom and tradition would go on for a long time yet under their own momentum—but, under the surface, it was insidious in its weakening effects on the sovereignty of the chiefs. It made them distrust one another more than ever; it sowed the seeds of distrust among their followers; it gradually sapped their own morale; it developed in them all the temper not of fight but of compromise; it increased the prestige of the Crown.

It annotates the position of religion in the story of the 16th century that it was not until a Catholic Queen came on the throne of England that this psychological infiltration was accompanied by anything serious in the way of conquest by force, though if all historians agree that in this Henry VIII was much more moderate in his dealings with Ireland than with England, he was so, no doubt,

SIR HUGH O'NEILL, EARL OF TYRONE, 1550 - 1616
Painted in exile by an unknown artist

for no better reason than that the Irish revenue was so far not worth more than a few thousand pounds a year. Under Mary two whole counties were confiscated and planted. The region of the Pale, about the puppet-parliament in Dublin, had found the O'Connors of Offaly and the O'Mores of Leix troublesome neighbours. Offaly and Leix were accordingly confiscated from the O'Connors and O'Mores and renamed King's County and Queen's County. So one blandly states the fact. The picture, as one might expect, is less one of plantation than of savage war to enforce the decision—a war that went on in those regions for almost fifty years, made horrible on all sides by repeated atrocities terrible even in a century when all warfare was of an extreme brutality whether in the Low Countries, or along the Spanish Main, or in the hills of Panama and Peru.

But it was under Elizabeth that the real war of conquest began. Here two great figures emerge, both of them men who had the intellect to clarify for the

23

bewildered Irish the situation into which the struggle of world forces had dragged them and their country. These were, firstly, James Fitzmaurice Fitzgerald, and secondly, Hugh O'Neill, Earl of Tyrone (1550 - 1616). Fitzgerald was the cousin of Gerald the 16th Earl of Desmond, and so of pure Norman extraction. O'Neill was a Gael of the Gaels. Fitzgerald was a zealot and an idealist fighting for all the pieties of the mediaeval world which had seen the founding of his line, calling to his aid Spain and Rome in the name of Christ and the universal Church, his motto set up on a banner wherever he camped—*In Omni Tribulatione et Angustia Spes Nostra Jesus et Maria.* O'Neill was a very different sort of man. He was the first Gaelic chief to embrace the Renaissance world, set firmly in limitless ambition, but shrewdly aware of all the rules of the dangerous game he played, open to every new idea, at first willing merely to use Religion, excited and inspired by it as he saw its cohesive and civilising power.

Fitzmaurice paved the way for O'Neill; indeed, he showed him the way. His "rising" is, perhaps, the first national "rebellion" in Irish history since, before his time, men were actuated more by personal considerations than by any large ideal. Fitzmaurice's uncle was the Earl of Desmond, at this time the accepted, traditional rival of the Earl of Ormond. On that long and deep-rooted rivalry a historical novelist might well base a great story of purely human ambition enlarged and ennobled by idealisms not so much embraced as embracing; for this is an era in which men are constantly becoming the creatures of things greater than themselves.

Desmond had never been a popular man. He was not strong and he had no charm and his illness had withheld him from the priceless education of courtly experience; the mingling with men; the analysis of political trends; the weighing of influence; prophecies, judgments, shrewd advices. Ormond, on the other hand, who had been the playmate of the child Elizabeth, was by nature an acute observer and a shrewd man-of-the-world, favoured in all and practised in all that Desmond lacked. Inevitably Desmond found himself, presently, under polite detention in London. He stayed there for year after year while, behind him, his people chafed, got out of hand, and finally became eager "rebels" when his cousin James Fitzmaurice declared that the Desmond rights were in danger, and raised not merely the flag of a just but, what was far more serious, of a Holy War. So began what is known to Irish history as the Desmond Rebellions; a series of now smouldering, now crackling disturbances that raced over the south of Ireland for fourteen years: from 1569 to 1583. Before they were quenched in blood they produced some savage incidents—such as occur in every war— which have ever since stood out from a welter of events (no less terrible in the aggregate) to define the basic antagonism in Irish history. One may say that modern Irish Nationalism begins with these incidents. The patriotic symbols begin to fill those niches which await them in the temple of every country's story.

At the side of Fitzmaurice, in the later stages of his desultory war, there stood two or three figures whose presence defines the enlargement of the issues. These were two Englishmen, the Papal Legate, Nicholas Sanders, and the Jesuit Father

ROCKINGHAM, NEAR BOYLE, CO. ROSCOMMON, BEFORE 1822

Built for Lord Lorton in 1810

Water colour probably by George Repton

NEAR RINGSEND, CO. DUBLIN

Early 19th century water colour by G. Holmes

Allen; and a Spaniard, Oviedo, also sent by Rome. Of these, Sanders was the great figure; a man of learning and a zealot, of tremendous character and of apparently irresistible magnetism. Without him the struggle would probably have fizzled out unheroically; for Fitzmaurice was killed soon after he returned to Ireland from a sojourn on the Continent (during a period of lull between 1573 and 1579). It was at this point that the palsied, vacillating, and harrassed Earl of Desmond, just come back from the misery of his London detention, fell into the hands either of God or Misfortune. Sanders, that is to say, now deprived of Fitzmaurice, turned to him and began to work upon him.

Desmond's weakness should have flung him into the safe arms of the English Government. It might have done so if the Government had not brutally demanded that he should stay where he was and fight for England. But his followers were the followers of his slaughtered cousin, Fitzmaurice, and all their natural, traditional loyalties were to Ireland and to the religion of their fathers. And, indeed, so were his own. The pressure of popular feeling, the pressure of Sanders' exhortations, the pressure of his own atavism so worked on him that, willy-nilly, he found his feeble, shivering body lifted on horseback, the cross placed in his hands, and behind him his people shouting triumphantly *Pápa Abú*—The Pope to Victory! Once again the rebellion was rationalised and moralised.

Spain presently sent an invading force to Kerry—in October, 1580. They found themselves besieged in a place called Dún-an-óir (The Fort of Gold) by Raleigh and Sidney, and were forced to the surrender. Six hundred of them were led out—"tall men" as the phrase of the time had it; meaning picked men. In the courtyard they were stabbed and slitted one by one and their white, naked bodies laid out in rows on the sands. Any women found in the place, some of them pregnant, were hanged. The incident is known as the Massacre of Smerwick.

Sanders died ultimately of hardship and fever. Nobody knows where. His bones mingle with some undeciphered corner of some quiet Munster field; he who had travelled through the courts of Europe, been honoured at the great centres of learning, rejected the ease of the study for the discomforts of hills that were not his own. It is about such names as his that we Irish most tenderly and emotionally weave the cere-cloths of memory—undying in its contact with honourable death. For it is our great strength to remember: as it is also, sometimes, our weakness. But it is our weakness only when we remember indiscriminately, as Irishmen too often do—less to foster wisdom than to kindle bitterness.

Desmond soon followed Sanders. Ruthless generals like Raleigh, Carew, and Perrot, burned Munster from end to end. In a great march down the peninsulas of Kerry each used to mark how the other progressed by the fires of the burning cabins glowing across the bays at night. By 1583 the whole South was a desert of tangled briars, wild grasses, and charred homesteads. More colonisation followed. English settlers were given grants of land of from 4,000 acres to 12,000 acres. Raleigh alone got 40,000 acres around Cork. The Crown was content with a modest quit-rent—in Kerry it amounted to a mere £100 for 12,000 acres. This aftermath of the Desmond Rebellions is known as "The Plantation of

Munster." The region thus planted was about one-fifth of the whole island. Put it with the plantation of Leix and Offaly (Queen's County and King's County) and we find that the government's radius out from Dublin strikes down now to the farthest south-westerly corner of the country, through the loyal lands of Ormond in Kilkenny. The reconquest of Ireland by the Tudors is going on apace.

Cantering beside Sidney in the early years of those Desmond wars was the young red-bearded Gaelic O'Neill known, then, as Baron of Dungannon. It marks the fissured nature of Irish society that this Gaelic O'Neill saw nothing odd in thus fighting for the Queen against Norman-Gaelic Fitzmaurice and his Catholic crusade. O'Neill, in any case, was too ambitious then to trouble about such fine points as loyalty to race or religion. His immediate aims were like that of every man about him—to gain power, to gain land, to gain followers, to spread, to become great. It was the spirit of the age, and as he had been reared as a boy in Sidney's household, and possibly in other great houses such as Leicester's he had swallowed whole this opportunistic spirit of the Elizabethan dare-devils and gamblers. This, too, we Irish sometimes tend to forget—that the Tudor aggressiveness was not directed with particular and exclusive animus against Ireland. Although the absolute control of the country was the state policy, it was really the impetuosity and greed of private adventurers that gave that policy its practical momentum; indeed it would often have lacked all animation without this incidental—one might almost say accidental drive of personal ambition. Men like the elder Essex, and indeed the younger Essex also, Raleigh, Carew, Mountjoy, Gilbert, Wingfield, Champernowne, Norris, St. Lawrence, Lee, Chichester, Bingham, were in the nature of lusty desperadoes whose willingness to take risks was encouraged by the Crown, whose experiments in bucaneering the Crown watched with a clinical interest, whose successes the Crown exploited, to whose personal failures the Crown could afford to be indifferent. The career of the elder Essex in Ireland was wholly of this irresponsible order. The Desmond Rebellions were fired in the first instance by a like irresponsible greed on the part of Sir Peter Carew of Mohun Ottery in Devon. There is in all this nothing surprising or, indeed, unusual. The methods and mentality of these gamblers were the methods and mentality of all young, eager, inventive, raw and ruthless peoples. An early familiarity with this farouche spirit of Renaissance England gave to Gaelic O'Neill, also, an opportunist twist, so that his part in the Desmond Rebellions was just as individualistic, reckless of larger consequences, and short-sighted as any. One has to stress this because he is the key-figure to those Irish wars of the 16th century, and his preoccupations reflect the times. The image of a united, patriotic, spirited nation resisting a cruel, deliberate invader thus proves—when tested by his behaviour, and he was the most patriotic Irishman of the century—to be far from a true picture.

Nevertheless the life of Hugh O'Neill shows *in petto* the slow emergence of that spirited national feeling. After the Desmond Rebellions he retired to the North to his own lands, claimed from the Crown his title of Earl of Tyrone, was

26

KERNS BURNING A HOUSE
Woodcut from John Derrick's *Image of Ireland*, 1581

granted it, and settled down to the business of consolidating his personal power. Had there been half-a-dozen men like him, scattered over the west, midlands, and north, it is highly probable that the history of Ireland would have been far different. These semi-feudal Gaelic chieftains, bearing English titles, solely for reasons of policy and not at all for reasons of affection, would have begun to take over the role of the earlier Norman Gaelic earls would, at least, have begun to rank with them, mingle with them, rival them, conspire with and against them, formed with England, as they had done, a loose, and no doubt always tricky *modus vivendi*—whose upshot would have depended on whether the Irish bear could or could not lie down with the English lion. But there, again, the religious motif comes in powerfully since both the old Anglo-Irish families and the Gaelic families were generally of the old persuasion, and as long as that question was held in the foreground there could have been no real peace. The Reformation was the crux in Anglo-Irish relations. (For an effort at some such sort of equitable compromise the student of Irish history might look at the so-called "Composition of Connaught" in 1585.)

The general hypothesis is not very helpful, however, since there were not six, or even two men like O'Neill. He was the one and only Gaelic chieftain with any sort of political acumen, with any sort of contemporary, international outlook. When, therefore, in the West the governor Bingham began, in his hot blood, to pound at the local chieftains there was no man there able to outwit him, as here in the North O'Neill was astute enough to outwit Bingham's counterpart, Bagenal. The western chiefs were of the order of border-raiders. They hacked and fled, and came back again like wasps, and tempers rose, and Bingham's blood

27

boiled hotter and hotter, and there gradually arose that exacerbated atmosphere which always surrounds antagonists who can sting but not defeat one another. English prestige was involved. The spirit of conquest flamed up again. Aggression having produced "rebellion"—odd word—the Crown had to support its deputy. To be sure, if the western chiefs had been clever enough to temporise with Bingham, as O'Neill was always temporising with Bagenal, they would have privately been able to increase their power, and so ham-strung him by their seeming compliance. But Bingham met no such politicians and, in any case, he was, by nature, a kind of bloodthirsty, roaring Timon calculated to drive any people beyond themselves; neither a wise governor nor an effective soldier.

Thus the wars approached O'Neill's northern strongholds via the west. Native fears were further roused by the Settlement of Monaghan in 1591, which, though it was far less ruthless than the Plantation of Munster, meant that the reigning chief was hanged, his son attainted, and all their lands taken over for subdivision among lesser chieftains by the Crown on its own terms. In the same year Red Hugh O'Donnell, the future chieftain of Tyrconnell (modern Donegal), escaped from long imprisonment in Dublin Castle, returned to the North, and stood ready to face the pressure that was shoving upwards to his borders from Bingham's centres in the West.

In this breathless tension the English government naturally turned for assistance to their own creation O'Neill, who, as Earl of Tyrone, had for years now (ever since the Desmond Rebellions) been holding himself as aloof as possible; but who, of course, in proportion as he succeeded in doing so was thereby the more suspected on all sides. He gradually found himself approaching the position of the Earl of Desmond of so many years before—caught in his own power by his dependence on his Gaelic followers, entangled in the suspicions of the Government, stiffened by his own pride, incited by a natural racial emotion which, with the years, had overgrown the effects of his youthful training in the English court. Perhaps it was this personal pride that affected him most; for he had seen the conquering wave creep up and up from the farthest south to his very door-step, was well aware that his power and wealth would always arouse envy among others, and saw no security except on terms that he must have considered too humiliating to be borne, and, even at that, could never be wholly relied on. Spanish and Papal emissaries were at his side; his neighbouring clansmen were urging him to fight; the Government nagged at him; and, at last, after prolonged delays, he threw down the sword in 1595.

That war went on until 1601, marked by some brilliant victories on his side, and an amazing incompetency on the side of the Crown. General after general fell before him, either to his sword or to his wily diplomacy. Essex was his most spectacular victim—and he and Essex hardly exchanged a single blow. A Spanish force landed, September, 1601, at Kinsale—the choice of place a grave error since it was in the remote South, and O'Neill was then being hard-pressed in the far North. These Spaniards were besieged in Kinsale for three months. Then O'Neill marched south, and besieged the besiegers. He was persuaded to give

SIEGE OF DUBLIN
Woodcut from Holinshed's *Chronicles of England, Scotlande and Irelande*, 1577

battle against his better judgment, and was utterly routed. He remained in arms until March, 1603, and then surrendered on honourable terms.

But the falcons were not to be foiled of their hawk. Deputies, government agents, land thirsty men of every kind, even churchmen, badgered him relentlessly. He realised that it would be only a matter of time before they trapped him, and his life would then end in the Tower. He and his immediate followers fled to Rome in 1607, and he died there in 1616. This departure into exile is known as the Flight of the Earls. Behind him the falcons tore the spoil to pieces; a sequel which is known as The Plantation of Ulster. It was not an utter extirpation. Many of the native chieftains remained for some time, much dwindled of course, and their position was rickety in the extreme. But though it was not possible to upset immediately, or thoroughly, the organised society of so vast a region, this Plantation virtually ended, for ever, the old Gaelic order. Other smaller Plantations followed both under James and Charles and there were wholesale and pitiless clearances under Cromwell. As they are all, in effect, the backwash of the Tudor wave of conquest it may be said, however, that it was under the Tudors that the old Gaelic world fell.

To look forward two centuries and more it is here that we see the sowing of the seed of the present-day problem of Irish Partition. After the Plantation of Ulster, a Colonist-Protestant life-mode became firmly established in the North-Eastern corner of the island, and the Catholic-Gaelic life-mode was firmly checked. The two races lived on side by side, nevertheless, in at least no greater tension

29

than one found elsewhere, all over the country, wherever a pocket of colonisation dominated the dispossessed about its demesne walls. Not until the middle of the last century did this tension become a threat anywhere in Ireland—and then but a weak one—to the continuing power of the colonists. As soon as it did, Protestant Ulster organised itself to defend what it had won, and so effectively and persistently that, as we see, to-day, the general emancipation of the island stops at the border of the Six Counties. It is, obviously, a difficult issue in which two forms of political realism face one another across the centuries. Its continuance has a considerable unsettling effect on present-day Anglo-Irish relationships.

The ultimate result of the Tudor conquest was that Ireland gradually became part of the English kingdom, ruled by English law, brought into line with English ways in so far as that could be where the people remained, on the whole, steadfastly Catholic, Gaelic speaking, devoted to the land from which their natural leaders had been driven out. The ultimate position is excellently summed up by Dr. Edmund Curtis (Professor of Modern History in the University of Dublin): "A new Irish nationality emerged, Catholic by conviction, a blend of English and Gael by race, and in the upper classes henceforth more and more English-speaking. But in the common people we see a blended race who in the long run have proved to be the characteristic Irish people, feeling a sense of common history and a common Faith, with an intense passion for the land which nothing has been able to shake, and speaking that Gaelic language which was the speech of the majority up to 1800. Milesian or Old English, Danish or Norman, whatever their origin they have all accepted the Irish legend as against the English legend. How to reconcile this Catholic nation, fast-forming because of a general ill-treatment, with an Anglican government was a problem, but how to make it fit in with a greedy, intolerant, and pampered aristocracy, which increased with every plantation, was a harder problem still."

The two great upheavals of the 17th century show how difficult that problem was. Twice in the seventy-five years between the death of O'Neill, Earl of Tyrone, and the beginning of the Penal Laws after the Williamite War, the country rose. And here one may properly speak, for the first time, of national uprisings. The first is known as the Insurrection of 1641, and men of every class and origin took part in it. The nationalist dogma was, however, far from clear. Some men fought for Religion, some for Land, some for the old Gaelic tradition, some for Charles I, some for the independence of a native parliament. The only unifying motto that emerged was *Pro Deo, pro Rege, pro Patria Hibernia unanimis*, and not everybody would have subscribed without reservations to that. This Insurrection was quenched in blood by the ever-to-be-execrated Cromwell, and was followed by a wholesale Confiscation to pay the Roundhead troops and adventurers.

From this period comes the phrase "To Hell or Connaught," commemorating the famous decision that after September, 1653, every Irish Catholic not judged to have held aloof from the insurrection, and owning property over the annual

SIEGE OF LONDONDERRY, 1689
Contemporary engraving

value of £10, must move westward across the river Shannon into the poor lands of Connaught: those permitted to stay east of the river must speak English and bring up their children as Protestants. Once again, however, vast numbers of the Catholic natives hung on about their old homes, dwindled now to the level of near-beggary, or intermarrying with the Cromwellians, so that to-day one constantly comes on those once-alien names that have blended happily with the traditional life-mode of the majority.

The second uprising (1685 - 1691) was also part-royalist, this time for James II against William. It ended with the Battle of the Boyne (July 1st, 1690) and the Siege of Limerick (September 4th to October 3rd, 1691). This war was followed immediately by an exodus to the Continent of about 12,000 of the flower of the Irish fighting-men, including almost all the remaining native aristocracy. This is the exodus known as The Flight of the Wild Geese and it marks the end, for all practical purposes, of that Gaelic, Catholic, aristocratic tradition which had now, within a hundred years, made three efforts to coagulate into a national movement: under O'Neill; in the Insurrection of 1641; and in the Williamite Wars.

Had these thousands remained at home, had leaders like Patrick Sarsfield, Earl of Lucan, returned to their estates, that tradition might not have died. As

31

it was there were still more confiscations—this time amounting to about one million acres. Nothing was left but the merest poor. Gaelic Ireland went underground with no other patrons than it found by cabin-fires under the leaky thatch or in the big houses of such few of the usurpers as tolerated it or vaguely sympathised with it. To be a Catholic now was to be an outlaw. The Treaty of Limerick had promised a far different state of affairs but it was violated both in the spirit and the letter. There begins what is sometimes known as The Bad Century, sometimes the Period of the Penal Laws, a hundred years of martyrdom out of which was to emerge modern Ireland.

THE BATTLE OF THE BOYNE, 1690
Contemporary engraving

THE story of Ireland up to the end of the 17th century is sufficiently savage and cruel and bloody. The word commonly used of Irish history, however, is not any one of these but "tragic." It was the 18th and 19th centuries that elicited this note of pity; the one because it was so utterly hopeless, a dismal despairing, defeated aftermath to a century of gallant resistance, the other because hope flickered more than once but was insufficiently nourished by the energy of Ireland and the conscience of England to make it live.

If one thinks of Irish history in terms of personalities, the 16th century is O'Neill's. For the seventeenth there is no symbolic figure unless we take O'Neill's nephew Owen Roe, or Lord Inchiquin, as the largest figures of the '41 Insurrection; or Patrick Sarsfield, Earl of Lucan, as the hero of the wars against William. But,

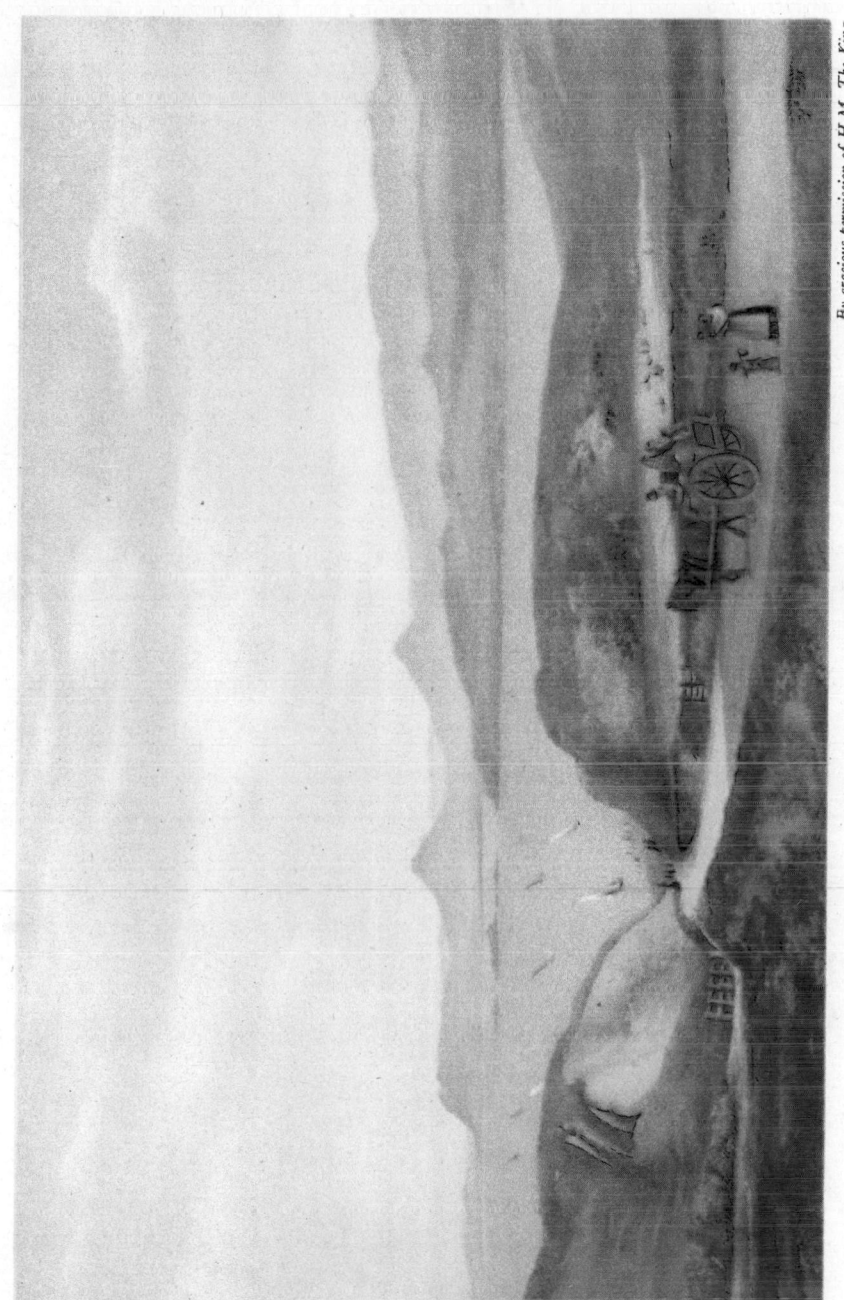

WICKLOW MOUNTAINS
Water colour by H. Newton, d. 1854

VIEW OF DUBLIN FROM PHOENIX PARK

Nineteenth century water colour

for the 18th century there is really no representative figure at all, since no public figure—neither Grattan, Wolfe Tone, nor Lord Edward Fitzgerald—spoke with the authority of the majority of the people. The explanation is simple; the mass of the people were reduced physically, mentally, and morally to the level of helots by a series of Acts of Parliament known as the Penal Laws. All commentators, from the Earl of Chesterfield to the great historian of the century, Lecky, agree as to the savagery of this legislation which, indeed, has the flavour of the Old Testament rather than of the Age of Enlightenment. These laws were passed at various times between 1696 and 1746. They were thoroughly inclusive. Under them no Catholic (*i.e.* the mass of the people) could sit in Parliament—he could not, as a matter of fact, even sit in the public gallery. He could not vote. He lost the municipal franchise. He could take no public office. His taxes were, in many cases, double that of his Protestant fellow. He could not lease land for more than thirty-one years nor make on it more profit than one-third of his rent. When he died his land was divided up among his sons. He could not enter the army. He could not possess a gun. He could not open a school. He could not own a horse valued more than £5: if he dared to do so any man could compel him to hand it over by tendering £5. All regular priests, all members of orders, and all dignitaries were deported. Intermarriage with Protestants was illegal. Orphans were handed over to Protestant guardians. There were many other similar ordinances, but the whole matter is adequately summed-up by the judge who declared from the bench in 1759 that the law did not presume a single Papist to breathe in Ireland.

It is difficult for us to understand how such inhuman laws could ever have been conceived; but it is well to remember that the Protestant Dissenters were also being persecuted under these laws—which to this day tends to keep them much closer to their Catholic fellows than to members of the (former) Established Church; and it is also to be remembered that many of these laws were copied from Louis XIV's contemporary decrees against the Huguenots. The Age of Reason was not an Age of Tolerance in any part of the globe.

Under this regime the people became utterly broken. They lived, for the greater part, in conditions of horrible misery. Their traditions were being taken from them; they had practically no means of education; they saw no hope of preferment for themselves or their generations. Chesterfield considered them treated worse than negroes, while Swift found them crushed; "harmless as women and children." Only abroad did they live—where the "Wild Geese" and their children won fame for Ireland in the armies of France, Spain, Austria, Italy, and America. The truly astonishing thing is that such a people ever rose again. That they did so is a tribute to their own toughness, in the first place, but it also means that the wars of the 16th and 17th centuries had welded together what had been, for so many centuries, a series rather than a society.

The island was not as a whole quite impassive. Swift, Dean of Saint Patrick's Cathedral from 1713 to 1745, wrote nobly and bitterly against the misgovernment of his adopted country. Later there arose a Protestant "Patriotic Party" led by men like Flood, Grattan, de Burgh, who blushed at the corruption of the Dublin parliament, and could not bear to see their country being exploited shamelessly for the benefit of the rising commercial classes in England. The Irish woollen trade had been ruined by an embargo on exportation in 1699. An Act of 1737 forbade the importation of any glass except from Britain, and an Act of 1746 forbade the exportation of any Irish glass at all. Under William and Anne an infant cotton industry was crushed by heavy duties. The provision trade was badly damaged by embargoes imposed between 1770 and 1780. Only one industry prospered—the manufacture of linen. Yet, in listing these misfortunes it is right to remember that it is to this period also that Ireland owes the beauty of most of her great houses throughout the country, and the splendid grace of the city of Dublin.

The Patriot Party finally won, in 1782, the legislative independence of their own Parliament in Dublin, so that laws were no longer subject to alteration or rejection by the English Privy Council under Poynings' Law. The result was, for a short period, a gratifying revival of industrial prosperity and a gradual relaxation of the more shameful interdictions on the Catholic mass of the population. As so often happens, however, this process was so slow and the concessions so niggardly that the spirit of revolt outpaced the spirit of reform: which is not surprising when we realise that no Catholics could yet sit in Parliament, and that no Catholic did, in fact, do so until after the first quarter of the 19th century.

This generous spirit of revolt did not, naturally, originate with the crushed mass of the people. It was in Belfast and among the Presbyterian Dissenters that the at first open, and later secret, Society of the United Irishmen was founded in 1791, aiming at "a brotherhood of affection and a communion of rights and a union of power among Irishmen of every religious persuasion"—an ideal obviously inspired by the French Revolution. The leading spirits in this republican movement were Theobald Wolfe Tone, in the North, and Lord Edward Fitzgerald, a brother of the Duke of Leinster, in the South. As a result of their activities a French expedition attempted a landing in 1796 but was blown off the coast; a small, and wholly local Rising broke out in 1798 and was crushed mercilessly; in August of the same year another French expedition landed in County Mayo, after the Rising had been crushed—that brief but gallant expedition was also quickly checked; in October Wolfe Tone himself sailed with a third, small French fleet to the North, was captured, condemned, and died in prison by his own hand.

These frightening events smoothened the way for the obliteration of the short-lived "Patriot Parliament," in the Legislative Union of the two islands. This Union, which was to create the United Kingdom of Great Britain and Ireland, had long been desired by the ruling junta in Dublin, best typified by the able but unscrupulous John Fitzgibbon, Earl of Clare, on the solid grounds that in no other way could the Protestant ascendancy and the security of the Empire be maintained in a country where three-fourths of the population—who must sooner or later get the franchise—were antipathetic to both. Pitt was of

THE UNITED IRISH PATRIOTS OF 1798
Contemporary engraving

the same opinion, with the assuaging addition that he was willing to extend the
franchise as soon as an Act of Union reduced the whole island to the safe condition
of a minority within a United Kingdom. By wholesale bribery and the shameless
distribution of peerages and profitable appointments the Irish Parliament was
finally induced to sign its own death-warrant. (In those undemocratic days the
mass of the people had, of course, no say in the matter: a few Catholics did possess
the vote, but the masses had none.) The Union became law on January 1, 1801,
and a new flag appeared on Dublin Castle—the saltire cross of Saint Patrick, red
on a white ground, joined with the cross of Saint George and Saint Andrew to
form what has become known as the Union Jack.

From the point of view of a brutal realism the Union was inevitable. It was
inherent in the Conquest, since the only alternative was sweeping reform, and
reform must, in giving power to the native majority, have undone the Conquest.
From the same point of view there was no justification for the Patriot Parliament
of 1782, and in practice (for the same reasons) it did not, and could not justify
itself. It was the parliament of a class, or party, not of a nation. But once the
Union was established, there was no longer any reason for not establishing a just
and natural polity in Ireland, and, in fact, the Union had been supported by

35

the bulk of the Catholic clergy—the only representatives the common people had—on the assumption, to which they had been led by specious promises, that the emancipation of their flock would immediately follow. In this they were grossly deceived.

With the Union, just as Dublin gradually ceased to be a centre of fashion and culture, the propertied minority gradually lost all status. The interest of the picture swings over to the common people and to the great figure of Daniel O'Connell who, from 1807, emerges as the dominant character in the Irish scene. Through a wholly constitutional society, the Catholic Association, he worked upon his vast army of helots, until by the colossal force of his personality, untiring energy, wily adaptability, legal ingenuity, floods of oratory, and an inexhaustible patience in organisation, he gradually lifted them out of their torpor, gave them hope and self-respect, discipline and self-reliance, until—though still without a single representative in Parliament—they became an irresistible force in imperial politics. Only a truly great man could have done it; and for greatness Balzac put O'Connell beside Napoleon, Cuvier—and Balzac.

He was, beyond question, the greatest agitator of all time. By levying on the people the sum of one farthing per week he amassed a powerful fighting fund, spread his clubs all over the country, sent his gospel into the most remote valleys, subsidised a newspaper, and gave his people a sound if elementary education in the technique of modern politics by which they have profited ever since. It was typical of his realism that he turned his back resolutely on Gaelic, although a Gaelic-speaker himself from the heart of Kerry. Indeed, by his modernism, his fluent opportunism, and his European outlook he resembles that much earlier leader, Hugh O'Neill; and it is significant that, like O'Neill, he, also, had been educated in London, whence he brought back the ideas and technique of the English Radicals, Godwin, Tom Paine, the French Deists, Adam Smith, Mary Wolstonecraft, Voltaire and Rousseau, to be assimilated, adapted, and put into words of one syllable for the peasants of Ireland.

His aim was Catholic Emancipation. His ideal was Liberty. Thus, when Emancipation came hopefully before Parliament in 1808 and the Irish bishops seemed ready to accept a government Veto on episcopal appointments, and when later, in 1814, the Pope himself, through the head of the Propaganda openly declared for the Veto, he denounced it outright, declaring that it would mean a Government partisan if not a Government informer in every parish. It took him twenty years to win his point; it was not until 1829 that Catholic Emancipation was finally granted.

There were, as usual, many niggling qualifications. One, incredibly, purported to suppress all monasteries and institutions of Jesuits. But the main result was of the first creative importance—it made possible a representative Irish Parliamentary Party. O'Connell slaved on, in and out of the Commons, for another fifteen years, agitating now for the Repeal of the Union; but he achieved little further and his end was tragic. He saw the Famine devour his country, kill off his people by the hundreds of thousands, and exile as many as it killed. In those

THE THOLSEL, DUBLIN
Aquatint from Malton's *Picturesque View of the City of Dublin*, 1791

years two-and-a-half million people were cleared out of Ireland, by famine, fever, or emigration. The curve persisted for two generations. By 1881 the population fell from eight millions to five.

Yet, Emancipation was only the outward achievement. O'Connell's real work was the elevation of his people, from their torpor, and their education in political technique. He left his mark indelibly on the national mind so that to understand fully the mentality of a modern Irishman it is necessary to study him. Above all he drew a clear line across tradition. Before 1800 inspiration had come from the Gaelic past: all through the 18th century, for example, the favourite theme of the wandering Gaelic poets was the return of the Stuarts, for whom Ireland had bled in the 17th century and with whom the first link had been forged by O'Neill in the 16th century. After O'Connell the people sought for leadership among themselves, and relied upon themselves, and thought for themselves as a modern democracy. He had in this sense defined the nature of modern Ireland, and in defining it he created it. The people saw their power clearly. They would envisage their future. All that remained for subsequent leaders was to continue and complete his work.

In the last years of O'Connell's life there had sprung up, side by side with his constitutional Repeal Movement, a young men's movement which was less

37

in his tradition of patient agitation than in the ardent revolutionary tradition of Wolfe Tone and the United Irishmen. This was the Young Ireland movement. The chief men in this movement were Thomas Davis, Gavan Duffy, Michael Doheny, John Mitchel. They worked with O'Connell but they privately feared and hated him. They were all able men of letters and their great contribution to Irish nationalism was its spirited expression in poems, songs, and essays; their best poet, James Clarence Mangan; their best prose-writer, John Mitchel. These men were idealists who created a brilliantly refracted picture of the past greatness of their country, which gave to the people that superflux of pride without which few can endure to the end. They created or gave wide currency to all those symbolic images which have ever since become the metaphorical language of Irish politics; Davis in particular went back eagerly to the Gaelic tradition which O'Connell rejected; they studied Irish history and, in their weekly paper, *The Nation*, brought back the people to its lessons again and again. Much of what they wrote was superficial—it is doubtful, for example, if Davis knew more than a few words of Gaelic, which was to him a prism rather than a lens—but it was always heroic and generous and uncompromising, and this was precisely the element that O'Connellism, with its coarser and more opportunist technique, inevitably lacked.

The truth is that the people were starving spiritually. There was not in any city, then, a street called after an Irishman—those commemorated were, instead, a Harcourt, a Sackville, an Essex, a Dorset, the instruments of official rule; whatever literature existed revelled chiefly in jokes about the stage-Irishman; no school-book on Irish history was used in any school; there was, in short, nothing visible in which any common Irishman could take pride. In all that spiritual desert the only oases were the songs of Tom Moore—how precious they must have been!—poems, probably little known, by men like Jeremiah Callanan, the speeches of O'Connell or Richard Lalor Shiel. Only those who lived in the remote Gaelic-speaking pockets possessed anything like a culture, and these were, by comparison, rich as Croesus. It is with these Young Irelanders that modern Anglo-Irish literature may be said to begin. They clothed Ireland in warm sentiment.

But their importance in the purely political history of Ireland is equally great—they carried on the tradition of resistance by arms. Driven mad by the spectacle of the Famine—during which, against all public appeals, the rich harvest of wheat and corn was sent to Britain or used to pay the landlords' rents—a handful of them tried to raise a rebellion in Munster in 1848, were arrested, deported, and so brought the Young Ireland movement to an end. The tradition was, however, too vital to die. It was carried on by the Fenians, James Stephens, O'Donovan Rossa, Charles Kickham, John O'Leary, some of whom lived on to our day— Yeats was a friend of old John Leary and was, in his youth, sworn into the Fenian movement—while the Irish Republican Brotherhood, founded in Dublin in 1858, as the fount and origin of Fenianism, was the backbone of the revolutionary Sinn Fein movement of the 1920's. In a residual, personal, disparate way its

DANIEL O'CONNELL, 1775 - 1847
A Vienna lithograph

influence probably still persists and will probably continue to persist for as long as its now-disbanded members live.

One has only to be in the company of a group of Irishmen, on a propitious occasion, for even an hour, to become aware of the persistence of the Young Ireland spirit on the emotional plane, and of the O'Connell tradition on the intellectual plane down to our own day. If some songs are sung a rise in the sentimental temperature is almost sure to indicate that *The Spirit of the Nation* (the anthology of Young Ireland verse), or some poet under its influence, is plucking again at the heart-strings. If there is, as there may well be, for the Irish nature turns as swiftly as a fish, a *volte face* into the ironical, the satirical, the sceptical, always, however, with its undercurrent of suppressed passion, it is the spirit of O'Connell—that passionate cryptographer—who broods over the gathering. Irishmen will probably never be free of the tyranny of that equivocating mind and the slavery of that emotional heart.

Men saw this bivalvular tradition at work in the great successor to O'Connell, Charles Stewart Parnell, with whom the Irish Parliamentary Party first became an effective reforming force. By means of it Parnell, in the House of Commons, and Davitt, in the Land League, won for Ireland an enormous amount of practical

39

liberty this side of autonomy. For whereas O'Connell left his people erect spiritually when he opened for them the gates of Emancipation but won practically nothing for them on the economic plane, before Parnell died they had won, or were obviously about to win, a real measure of control over their own affairs.

Already before his entry to power, the first Land Act (1870) had pointed the direction of their economic emancipation. The Secret Ballot Act (1872), which made the peasants independent at the polls of landlord interference, confirmed the pointer. His constitutional agitation in Parliament, and Michael Davitt's more forceful methods in the Land League, brought home further reforms. Thus the Land Bill of 1881 established the tenant's rights; it fixed his rent, and prevented a landlord from practising any longer that bad trick of increasing the rent whenever a tenant, by his own industry, improved the value of his holding. The Franchise Act of 1884 extended Household Suffrage to Ireland and thus made electors of the labourer and artisan. In 1885 the Ashbourne Act lent the farmers five million pounds at four per cent. for the purchase of their land, over a period of forty-nine years' repayment: the Land Purchase Bill of 1891 increased this sum to thirty millions. If these reforms should not strike the reader as being of major importance he must remember that to our forefathers they made all the difference between slavery and a tolerable existence. Every one of them was the creak of a jack lifting from their backs an intolerable burthen.

Further legislation, such as Balfour's Land Act of 1896, or the Local Government Act of 1898, continued this work after the death of Parnell. That 1898 Act created a virtual revolution in Irish life: it abolished the Grand Jury system and gave to the common people, through the County Councils, a considerable amount of local administrative power and responsibility. The Irish historian Haverty says of this reform that all the people now lacked was University Education and that "if the latter were once granted the Conservatives would have nothing left to grant but Home Rule." (This University question was finally solved in 1908 when the Royal University, founded 1879, was abolished and two new popular universities were established—Queen's University, Belfast, with a single college, and the National University of Ireland with three colleges—in Dublin, Cork, and Galway.)

There were many other reforms, such as Church Disestablishment; the founding of a widespread Primary Education scheme (popularly spoken of as "The National Schools"); a Land Purchase Act of 1903, which was known as the Wyndham Act, advanced a further hundred million pounds to the small farmers at favourable terms; a Department of Agriculture and Technical Instruction was set up under Horace Plunkett and still functions. If one looks back, with all this in mind, to the condition of the country before the rise of O'Connell, one has to agree that a great part of the misery inherent in the original Conquest was gradually being undone. Indeed, by 1910 or so, any acute observer with a fair knowledge of Irish history, and a capacity to assess the general trend, might have been able to say that the final reform of Home Rule, in some shape or other, was an absolute certainty—as certain as it is to-day for India.

W. B. YEATS, 1865-1939

Oil painting by Augustus John

JAMES STEPHENS
Oil painting by Sir William Rothenstein

CORK FROM THE MARDYKE WALK
Aquatint from J. Carr's *The Stranger in Ireland*, 1806

But while one can, now, write dispassionately about Irish history from the Famine to the death of Parnell, there was nothing dispassionate about Anglo-Irish relations during those fifty odd years. Every single reform was not so much granted as wrested. They were accompanied by frequent bloodshed, and more than frequent coercion. Many Members of Parliament, from Parnell down, were jailed during those hectic years—some, like the famous Member for Cork, William O'Brien, as often as five times. The Land Question was fought with particular bitterness; which is not surprising seeing that in a country so exclusively agricultural it was the foremost problem. Indeed, Isaac Butt, Parnell's predecessor, once declared that it formed the "whole problem." Here the landlords resisted tooth and nail; so that Lord Beaconsfield had gone so far as to stigmatise Gladstone's wholly tentative effort of 1881 as "legalised confiscation"—although it proposed little more than that the farmer's rent should be fixed judicially and that, under certain conditions, he might take out a lease. It was the familiar impasse of the statesman who is willing, blocked by the vested interest that is most obstinately not.

The final stage of the modern history of the United Kingdom of Great Britain and Ireland was, in this sense, a race against time. By 1914 Home Rule was on the Statute Book—to be conferred after the War; subject, however, to probable revision. Could it have been granted then the emergent Sinn Fein movement would probably have petered out, or, at any rate would have merged into a constitutional movement within the Irish Parliament. To be more precise, Home Rule (if Sinn Fein was to be forestalled) should have been granted just one year earlier—in 1913; for that was the crucial year in modern Irish politics. It was the year in which Sir Edward Carson founded the Ulster Volunteers with the

41

avowed aim of fighting Home Rule with the gun. He set the example to the South which at once turned the political movement of Sinn Fein into the armed movement of the Irish Volunteers. 1913 was also the restless year of the great Dublin Tramway Strike out of which emerged another armed force, the Irish Citizen Army. What that means, in effect, is that the Young Ireland tradition of revolutionary politics was leaning across the O'Connell tradition of constitutional politics and appealing to the old, deep-rooted emotional thing, to old memories and old symbols whose force grew and grew in proportion as hope was deferred.

The rising graph of Sinn Fein ambitions indicates as much. At first its "Father," Arthur Griffith, later first President of the Irish Free State, was content to ask in his paper *The United Irishman* (it came out in 1899) for the restoration of the "Patriot Parliament" of 1782, complete with the King, Lords, and Commons of Ireland. In 1900 he advocated, as the means of winning this, abstention from the English House of Commons, and internal agitation, in imitation of the technique of the Magyar leader, Deak—as later outlined by Griffith in his book *The Resurrection of Hungary*. In 1905 he had collected his adherents into a National Council. Then the Irish Republican Brotherhood took a hand, and in 1907, gathered together every little organisation at all savouring of the Left into an active nation-wide network of local clubs. In these, under the influence of the Brotherhood, Republicanism began to replace the monarchist Constitution of 1782. By 1911 the Brotherhood had become impatient and founded their own paper *Irish Freedom*, chiefly because Griffith was not willing to be extreme in his demands. Labour unrest in the same year excited the public mind. The Unionist Clubs and the Orange Lodges were passing violent resolutions against Asquith and the Liberals. Then came the big Dublin strike of 1913, and the temperature rose rapidly. John Redmond, the successor of Parnell, found himself obliged to sponsor the Irish Volunteers, that armed movement which was the southern riposte to Carson's Ulster Volunteers. Griffith was still willing to accept a moderate Home Rule, and Pearse, the leader of the 1916 Rising in Dublin, was in those years prepared to fall into line with Griffith.

At first the outbreak of war seemed not only to cut across this graph but to blot it out completely. Redmond at the outbreak of the war offered the Irish Volunteers for the defence of the Empire. Thousands upon thousands at once joined the British Army. (The Irish Ex-Servicemen's Legion computes that 50,000 Irish were killed in France and Flanders.) The 1916 Rising was thus totally unexpected by the majority of the people. It was, in fact, a colossal gamble by the extreme wing of the Sinn Fein—I.R.B. movement: a gallant, but apparently hopeless appeal by that old Young Ireland tradition to submerged loves and forgotten hates. It is a matter of history that, as far as immediate results are concerned, the Rising failed in this: it did not touch the spark until the leaders began to march, one by one, before the firing-squads. Then the whole magazine of long-buried emotions blew up under the feet of the constitutional politicians. Even still Home Rule, granted promptly, might have saved both Ireland and Great Britain a great deal of later unhappiness. Instead an Irish Convention,

CHARLES STEWART PARNELL, 1846 - 1891
Cartoon by *T.* in *Vanity Fair*, 1880

called together by Mr. Lloyd George, petered out ineffectually. It had met in the odour of martyred blood.

That was 1917-1918. By 1920 Parliamentarianism was finished. In 1922, after several years of bloodshed, Ireland was offered what used to be called "Home Rule," and was now—in the geared-up symbolism of those bloody years—called Independence. Griffith, who had always known his own moderate mind, accepted. De Valera, whose whole life had been inspired by the Young Ireland spirit, refused. A bitter Civil War followed. Griffith died. Michael Collins, the foremost figure in those revolutionary years, was killed. But the "Irish Free State" weathered the storm, and its Dail (or Parliament) was now functioning. At first De Valera tried the old abstentionist technique, but after a few years he found that the old symbols were blunted, the people tired, and idealism at a low ebb. He entered the Free State Dail, gradually built up his influence afresh, in 1932 won his majority, and took over the Government. Many reasons are given for his success. One factor which helped him back to power was public unrest arising from the 1929 Depression.

Under him Anglo-Irish relations may not, on the surface, appear to be as cordial as they were under President Griffith and President Cosgrave. That impression arises for three reasons. The first was an argument about money, and nothing else was involved. This is known as the dispute about the Land Annuities. These, to put the thing simply, constitute the interest on those previously-mentioned large loans for land-purchase plus the annual repayment quota: the money went, ultimately, to pay the British Government, who paid the landlords who had been bought out. The Irish Government claimed that it was no part of the agreed settlement of 1922 that these Annuities should go to Great Britain, and withheld them. The British Government recouped itself for their loss by placing tariffs on Irish exports, chiefly cattle. The dispute—which involved some £5 millions a year, or a capital sum of £100 millions—was settled when the Irish Government compounded by a payment of ten million pounds.

The second dispute was of far larger import. It concerned the constitutional rights of Ireland in relation to the British Commonwealth of Nations. Here the Irish position is that it is a co-equal and freely associated nation, with a sovereignty unqualified as to internal affairs, and as to external affairs qualified only by the natural obligations inherent in any such free association. Mr. De Valera brought this matter to the foreground by abrogating the first Constitution of the Irish Free State and drawing up a Constitution which the British Government has refused to approve.

Constitutional lawyers have written a great deal on this dispute but I think one of the simplest summaries is that of Henry Harrison, in his book *Ireland and the British Empire*. He puts the British view-point as follows. Having pointed out that the sovereignty of Ireland in external matters is qualified by a common allegiance to the Crown he goes on to say: "The quality of the allegiance to the Crown has not been authoritatively defined . . . It is a constitutional crown and of symbolic import. It carries with it no unexpended prerogative beyond the

CUSTOM HOUSE, DUBLIN
Aquatint from J. Carr's *The Stranger in Ireland*, 1806

control of Dominion legislatures." While the Crown is not thus a warrant of external authority, and its powers rest on the Dominion constitution—alterations as regards succession, for example, as we saw at the time of the abdication of Edward VIII, require the consent of all members of the Commonwealth—he agrees, nevertheless, that the symbolic value of the Crown is paramount. The difficulty is that this value eludes the definition of a merely formal phraseology. It would appear that everything here depends, much as in a family, on custom, need, trust, propinquity, and, especially, the unchallenged independence of each member. When the present war broke out Great Britain and Ireland were still intermittently engaged in this constitutional argument, probing one another for definitions of (a) corporate obligations, and (b) individual rights; which inevitably implies a relationship which one can more easily think of as subtle rather than cordial. The War has produced the main reason for thinking so. Since Eire's immediate and personal concern was directed towards her individual rights, rather than to the question of corporate obligations, it was not surprising that she should assert her right to remain neutral.

To-day Eire's neutrality has the proportions of a major question, if not of a crucial question, in Anglo-Irish relations. It would be very short-sighted to divorce it from the long series of events which have led us up to it, and which must lead us onward from it. In this brief survey we have withdrawn, in relation to all other events, to a very distant perspective in order to get a very large scene into a small finder. At that perspective the major events stand out clearly, and a great many other events—many of which appeared at the time to be crucial—drop away into comparative unimportance. So it may be with Eire's present international problems. The passage of time is constantly introducing new circumstances into every historical scene, and each one of these new circumstances is capable of altering radically the emphasis of the whole composition—a process which does not cease until a period completes itself and becomes framed-off, after which new events begin to cluster about another nucleus. So far Eire's Neutrality is the asseveration of a right, not of an intention. It depends on future statesmen to understand this; to realise that it is a negative action, not a positive action; that this constitutional tension is as old as the Normans; that it is the warp and woof of the Story of Ireland; to remember, on looking back, how much unhappiness might have been spared had more human understanding and more patience been shown on both sides; and, on looking forward, to acknowledge how much these qualities may spare us all in the future.

This also must be said. The outstanding thing that emerges in this record is the rise, in Ireland, of a growing democratic intelligence. In the period of Hugh O'Neill the common people counted for far less than in our day; they co-operated inadequately with O'Neill because they hardly understood at all what was involved. In the Confederation of 1641 they co-operated a little better because the picture was becoming a little more clear to them. In the days of O'Connell they co-operated whole-heartedly because, as a Man of the People, he made them understand fully. This implication of a dichotomy in Irish life between the "people" and some others not of the people is realistic. Some time in 1942 the Mayor of Courbevoie introduced some young craftsmen to Marshal Petain as "children of the people." "Why do you speak of them as children of the people?" asked the Marshal. "Are they not Frenchmen? Say that they come from working-class families if you like, but please don't say 'children of the people' since we all belong to the same people." The reproof may be valid in France. In Ireland it would not be valid, since what emerged out of the Conquest and its undoing was a genuine democracy. Observers of Ireland should always remember this, and realise that the public intelligence of Ireland is the intelligence of an historic nexus of simple folk with a long and tragic struggle behind them. It is their emotional reactions and their instinctive loyalties that count. It is to these that O'Connell appealed; and Wolfe Tone, who described them gaily as "that large and respectable class, the men of no property." It is these who flocked behind Parnell, and Davitt, and Michael Collins. What they may be thinking at any moment it is difficult for any statesman, or any observer, to say. But one feels that there is something in one people that understands another; an element of sympathy which is infrequently present to the same degree in statesmen and politicians. And as one Irishman who wishes that Anglo-Irish relations should be of the most friendly I think that nothing is more important, and more often neglected, than that there should, for this reason, be close contact between the common folk of Ireland and the common folk of Great Britain. For, too often, the story of Ireland is presented to both in purely subjective terms; some of the

A CONNAUGHT FISHING VILLAGE
Oil painting by Paul Henry

most fantastic order such as "loyalty" and "rebellion," on the one hand; or, in Ireland, with a whole vocabulary of emotional appeals that might lead any stranger to conclude that we Irish have some kind of instinctive abhorrence for Englishmen as such, or that there is something inherently unique in the nature of our problem. Whereas the story of Ireland is, in its first part the common story of a conquest undertaken, basically, for material reasons, and, in its second part, the story of the gradual undoing of that material conquest. The revolution which began with O'Connell was thus a social revolution, at bottom, and continued to be so all through the Land War of the 19th century under Davitt and Parnell. Thus it is significant that the Redmond - Lloyd George Convention broke on the Fiscal Question; as it is interesting that Mr. De Valera's first dispute with the British Government was on the old question of those Land Annuities. I venture to say that, to-day, the mass of the people are far more interested in social problems than in constitutional problems and that it may well be a considerable danger to Mr. De Valera's continuing influence that he is more adept at the latter than

47

at the former. It should be made clear, however, that on the constitutional position the mass of the people are whole-heartedly behind De Valera.

But every society is informed by its own ideals, as well as motivated by its own necessities. Once the common people passed the border-line of economic insecurity—which they did only within this century—they began to consider what images of life were not merely bearable but desirable. They are still thinking that out, and will go on thinking it out for a very long time to come—perhaps for generations. All the controversies which now engage public attention in Ireland are directed towards these social, cultural, and moral questions, so that it generally happens that problems are tackled equally from the point of view of political philosophy and objective expediency: as with education, for example, in which the revival of Gaelic is less ardently debated as an educational question than as a question of national honour; or as with Economic policy which is considered as much in the light of national pride as in the light of national prosperity. At the moment, therefore, the whole set-up of Irish life is this tension between inarticulate desire and the pressure of circumstances, and the one thing the people feel is that they need to work out their destiny as undisturbed as may be—a most natural desire when one realises that they have been waiting through several centuries for the opportunity. Nothing has done so much to foster friendly Anglo-Irish relations as the discovery that Great Britain, even in her greatest need, has not done anything to interfere with that process of nation-building, and nothing will continue to foster those friendly relations so effectively as the growing assurance—not easy to inculcate, as one might expect from all that has gone before—that the Irish people are permanently free to create the life-modes that they consider most suited to their national genius.

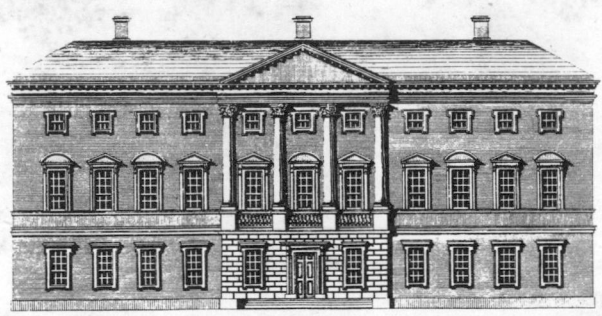

THE WEST FRONT OF LEINSTER HOUSE IN 1780
Now Dail Eireann